The Crescent Moon Book
of Metaphysical Poetry

POETRY FROM CRESCENT
MOON

Walking In Cornwall
by Ursula Le Guin

Hymns To the Night
by Novalis

*Hymns To the Night: In
Translation*
by Novalis

*Flower Pollen: Selected
Thoughts*
by Novalis

*Novalis: His Life, Thoughts
and Works*
by Novalis

Edmund Spenser: *Heavenly
Love: Selected Poems*
selected and introduced by
Teresa Page

Edmund Spenser: *Amoretti*
edited by Teresa Page

*The Visions of Petrarch and
Bellay: Early Sonnets*
by Edmund Spenser

Percy Bysshe Shelley:
*Paradise of Golden Lights:
Selected Poems*
selected and introduced by
Charlotte Greene

Robert Herrick: *Delight In
Disorder: Selected Poems*
edited and introduced by
M.K. Pace

Robert Herrick: *Hesperides*
edited and introduced by
M.K. Pace

Robert Herrick: *Upon Julia's
Breasts: Love Poems*
edited and introduced by
M.K. Pace

Sir Thomas Wyatt: *Love For
Love: Selected Poems*
selected and introduced by
Louise Cooper

John Donne: *Air and Angels:
Selected Poems*
selected and introduced by
A.H. Ninham

D.H. Lawrence: *Being Alive:
Selected Poems*
edited with an introduction by
Margaret Elvy

D.H. Lawrence: *Amores*
edited with an introduction by
Margaret Elvy

D.H. Lawrence: *Look! We
Have Come Through!*
edited with an introduction by
Margaret Elvy

D.H. Lawrence: *Love Poems and Others*
edited with an introduction by Margaret Elvy

D.H. Lawrence: *New Poems*
edited with an introduction by Margaret Elvy

D.H. Lawrence: *Symbolic Landscapes*
by Jane Foster

D.H. Lawrence: *Infinite Sensual Violence*
by M.K. Pace

Thomas Hardy: *Her Haunting Ground: Selected Poems*
edited, with an introduction by A.H. Ninham

Thomas Hardy: *Late Lyrics and Earlier*
edited, with an introduction by A.H. Ninham

Thomas Hardy: *Moments of Vision*
edited, with an introduction by A.H. Ninham

Thomas Hardy: *Poems of the Past and the Present*
edited, with an introduction by A.H. Ninham

Thomas Hardy: *Satires of Circumstance*
edited, with an introduction by A.H. Ninham

Thomas Hardy: *Time's Laughingstocks*
edited, with an introduction by A.H. Ninham

Thomas Hardy: *Wessex Poems*
edited, with an introduction by A.H. Ninham

Sexing Hardy: Thomas Hardy and Feminism
by Margaret Elvy

Emily Bronte: *Darkness and Glory: Selected Poems*
selected and introduced by Miriam Chalk

John Keats: *Bright Star: Selected Poems*
edited with an introduction by Miriam Chalk

John Keats: *Poems of 1820*
edited with an introduction by Miriam Chalk

Henry Vaughan: *A Great Ring of Pure and Endless Light: Selected Poems*
selected and introduced by A.H. Ninham

Arthur Rimbaud: *Selected Poems*
edited and translated by Andrew Jary

Arthur Rimbaud: *A Season in Hell*
edited and translated by Andrew Jary

Canzoniere
by Francesco Petrarch

Friedrich Hölderlin: *Hölderlin's Songs of Light: Selected Poems*
translated by Michael Hamburger

Rainer Maria Rilke: *Dance the Orange: Selected Poems*
translated by Michael Hamburger

Rainer Maria Rilke: *Poems*
translated by Jessie Lamont

Auguste Rodin
by Rainer Maria Rilke

Rilke: Space, Essence and Angels In the Poetry of Rainer Maria Rilke
by B.D. Barnacle

German Romantic Poetry: Goethe, Novalis, Heine, Hölderlin
by Carol Appleby

The North Sea
by Heinrich Heine

Rampoli: Poems From Mainly German
by George Macdonald

Arseny Tarkovsky: *Life, Life: Selected Poems*
translated by Virginia Rounding

Emily Dickinson: *Wild Nights: Selected Poems*
selected by Miriam Chalk

Delia
by Samuel Daniel

Idea
by Michael Drayton

Astrophil and Stella
by Sir Philip Sidney

Elizabethan Sonnet Cycles
by Daniel, Drayton, Sidney, Spenser and Shakespeare

Elizabethan Sonnet Cycles (Volume Two)
by Lodge, Griffin, Smith, Constable and Fletcher

Three Metaphysical Poets
edited by A.H. Ninham

Three Romantic Poets
edited by Miriam Chalk

The Crescent Moon Book
of Metaphysical Poetry

Edited by Charlotte Greene

CRESCENT MOON

CRESCENT MOON PUBLISHING
P.O. Box 1312, Maidstone
Kent, ME14 5XU
Great Britain
www.crmoon.com

First published 1996. Second edition 2008. Third edition 2016.
Pocket Edition 2022.
Introduction © Charlotte Greene, 1996, 2008, 2016, 2022.

Set in Times New Roman 9 on 12 pt.
Designed by Radiance Graphics.

The right of Charlotte Greene to be identified as the editor of this
book has been asserted generally in accordance with sections 77
and 78 of the Copyright, Designs and Patents Act 1988.

British Library Cataloguing in Publication data

ISBN-13 9781861711373
ISBN-13 9781861715302
ISBN-13 9781861718501

Contents

JOHN DONNE
(1572-1631)

Love's Alchemy

SOME THAT have deeper digged love's mine than I,
Say, where his centric happiness doth lie:
      I have loved, and got, and told,
But should I love, get, tell, till I were old,
I should not find that hidden mystery;
      Oh, 'tis impostur all:
And as no chemic yet the elixir got,
      But glorifies his pregnant pot,
      If by the way to him befall
Some odoriferous thing, or medicinal,
  So, lovers dream a rich and long delight,
  But get a winter-seeming summer's night.

Our ease, our thrift, our honour, and our day,
Shall we, for this vain bubble's shadow pay?
      Ends love in this, that my man,
Can be as happy as I can; if he can
Endure the short scorn of a bridegroom's play?
      That loving wretch that swears,

'Tis not the bodies marry, but her angelic finds,
　　　Would swear as justly, that he hears,
In that day's rude hoarse minstrelsy, the spheres.
Hope not for mind in women; at their best
　　Sweetness and wit, they are but mummy, possessed.

Song: Go and Catch a Falling Star

GO AND catch a falling star,
   Get with child a mandrake root,
Tell me, where all past years are,
   Or who cleft the devil's foot,
Teach me to hear mermaids singing,
   Or to keep off envy's stinging,
        And find
        What wind
Serves to advance an honest mind.

If thou be'est born to strange sights,
   Things invisible to see,
Ride ten thousand days and nights,
   Till age snow white hairs on thee,
Thou, when thou return'st, wilt tell me
All strange wonders that befell thee,
        And swear
        No where
Lives a woman true, and fair.

If thou find'st one, let me know,
   Such a pilgrimage were sweet,
Yet do not, I would not go,
   Though at next door we might meet,
Though she were true, when you met her,

And last, till you write your letter,
        Yet she
        Will be
False, ere I come, to two, or three.

Negative Love

I NEVER stooped so low, as they
Which on an eye, cheek, lip, can prey,
    Seldom to them, which soar no higher
    Than virtue or the mind to admire,
For sense, and understanding may
    Know, what gives fuel to their fire:
My love, though silly, is more brave,
For may I miss, whene'er I crave,
If I know yet what I would have.

If that be simply perfectest
Which can by no way be expressed
    But negatives, my love is so.
    To all, which all love, I say no.
If any who decipher best,
    What we know not, ourselves, can know,
Let him teach me that nothing; this
As yet my ease, and comfort is,
Though I speed not, I cannot miss.

To Mr C.B.

THY FRIEND, whom thy deserts to thee enchain,
   Urged by this inexcusable occasion,
   Thee and the saint of his affection
Leaving behind, doth of both wants complain;
And let the love I bear to both sustain
   No blot nor maim by this division,
Strong is this love which ties our hearts in one,
And strong that love pursued with amorous pain;
But though besides thyself I leave behind
   Heaven's liberal, and earth's thrice-fairer sun,
   Going to where stern winter aye doth won,
Yet, love's hot fires, which martyr my sad mind,
   Do send forth scalding sighs, which have the art
   To melt all ice, but that which walls her heart.

from *Divine Meditations*

1

I AM a little world made cunningly
Of elements, and an angelic sprite,
But black sin hath betrayed to endless night
My world's both parts, and, oh, both parts must die.
You which beyond that heaven which was most high
Have found new spheres, and of new lands can write,
Pour news seas in mine eyes, that so I might
Drown my world with my weeping earnestly,
Or wish it if it must be drowned no more:
But oh it must be burnt; alas the fire
Of lust and envy have burnt it heretofore,
And made it fouler; let their flames retire,
And burn me O Lord, with a fiery zeal
Of thee and thy house, which doth in eating heal.

AT THE round earth's imagined corners, blow
Your trumpets, angels, and arise, arise
From death, you numberless infinities
Of souls, and to your scattered bodies go,
All whom the flood did, and fire shall o'erthrow,
All whom war, earth, age, agues, tyrannies,
Despair, law, chance, hath slain, and you whose eyes,
Shall behold God, and never taste death's woe.
But let them sleep, Lord, and me mourn a space,
For, if above all these, my sins abound,
'Tis late to ask abundance of thy grace,
When we are there' here on this lowly ground,
Teach me how to repent; for that's as good
As if thou hadst sealed my pardon, with thy blood.

from Holy Sonnets

Annunciation

SALVATION TO all that will is nigh,
That all, which always is all everywhere,
Which cannot sin, and yet all sins must bear,
Which cannot die, yet cannot choose but die,
Lo, faithful virgin, yields himself to lie
In prison, in thy womb; and though he there
Can take no sin, nor thou give, yet he 'will wear
Taken from thence, flesh, which death's force may try.
Ere by the spheres time was created, thou
Wast in his mind, who is thy son, and brother,
Whom thou conceiv'st, conceived' yea thou art now
Thy maker's maker, and thy father's mother,
Tho' hast light in dark; and shutt'st in little room,
Immensity cloistered in thy dear womb.

Ascension

SALUTE THE last and everlasting day,
Joy at the uprising of this sun, and son,
Ye whose just tears, or tribulation
Have purely washed, or burnt your drossy clay;
Behold the highest, parting hence away,
Lightens the dark clouds, which he treads upon,
Nor doth he by ascending, show alone,
But first he, and he first enters the way.
O strong ram, which hast battered heaven for me,
Mild lamb, which with thy blood, hast marked the path;
Bright torch, which shin'st, that I the way may see,
Oh, with thine own blood quench thine own just wrath,
And if thy holy Spirit, my Muse did raise,
Deign at my hands this crown of prayer and praise.

LADY MARY WROTH
(*c.* 1586-*c.*1632)

Sonnet XIX

COME DARKEST night, becoming sorrow best;
    Light, leave to thy light, fit for a lightsome soul;
    Darkness doth truly suit with me oppressed,
    Whom absence' power doth from mirth control:
The very trees with hanging heads condole
    Sweet summer's parting, and of leaves distressed
    In dying colours make a griefful roll,
    So much, alas, to sorrow are they pressed.
Thus of dead leaves her farewell carpet's made:
    Their fall, their branches, all their mournings prove,
    With leafless, naked bodies, whose hues vade
    From hopeful green, to wither in their love:
If trees and leaves for absence mourners be,
No marvel that I grieve, who like want see.

ROBERT HERRICK
(1591-1674)

To Find God

WEIGH ME the fire; or canst thou find
A way to measure out the Wind;
Distinguish all those Floods that are
Mix'd in that watrie theatre;
And taste thou them as saltlesse there
As in their channel first they were.
Tell me the People that do keep
Within the Kingdoms of the Deep;
Or fetch me back that Cloud again
Beshiver'd into seeds of Rain;
Tell me the motes, dust, sands, and spears
Of corn, when Summer shakes his ears;
Show me that world of Starres, and whence
They noiseless spill their Influence:
This if thou canst, then show me Him
That rides the glorious *Cherubim*.

On Heaven

PERMIT MINE eyes to see
Part, or the whole of Thee,
    O happy place!
    Where all have Grace,
    And Garlands shar'd,
    For their reward;
    Where each chaste Soul
    In long, white stole,
    And Palmes in hand,
    Do ravisht stand;
    So in a ring,
    The praises sing
    Of Three in One,
    That fill the Throne;
While Harps, and Viols then
To Voices, say, *Amen.*

Eternitie

O YEARS! and Age! Farewell:
        Behold I go,
        Where I do know
Infinitie to dwell.

And these mine eyes shall see
        All times, how they
        Are lost i'th'Sea
Of vast Eternitie.

Where never Moone shall sway
        The Starres; but she,
        And Night, shall be
Drown'd in one endlesse Day.

Life Is the Body's Light

LIFE IS the body's light; which, once declining,
Those crimson clouds i' th' cheeks and lips leave
                                    shining:-
Those counter-changed tabbies in the air,
The sun once set, all of one colour are:
So, when death comes, fresh tinctures lose their
                                    place,
And dismal darkness then doth smutch the face.

The Eye

MAKE ME a heaven; and make me there
Many a less and greater spheare.
Make me the straight, and oblique lines;
The Motions, Lations, and the Signes.
Make me a Chariot, and a Sun;
And let them through a Zodiac run:
Next, place me Zones, and Tropicks there;
With all the Seasons of the Yeare.
Make me a Sun-set; and a Night:
And then present the Mornings-light
Cloath'd in her Chamlets of Delight.
To these, make Clouds to poure downe raine;
With weather foule, then faire againe.
And when, wise Artist, that thou hast,
With all that can be, this heaven grac't;
Ah! what is then this curious skie,
But only my *Corinna's* eye?

GEORGE HERBERT

(1593-1632)

The Starre

BRIGHT SPARK, shot from a brighter place,
  Where beams surround my Saviours face,
   Canst thou be any where
    So well as there?

Yet, if thou wilt from thence depart,
  Take a bad lodging in my heart;
   For thou canst make a debter,
    And make it better.

First with thy fire-work burn to dust
  Folly, and worse then folly, lust:
   Then with thy light refine,
    And make it shine.

So disengag'd from sinne and sicknesse,
  Touch it with thy celestiall quicknesse,
   That it may hang and move
    After thy love.

Then with our trinitie of light,
    Motion, and heat, let's take our flight
        Unto the place where thou
            Before didst bow.

Get me a standing there, and place
    Among the beams, which crown the face
        Of him, who dy'd to part
            Sinne and my heart:

That so among the rest I may
    Glitter, and curle, and winde as they:
        That winding is their fashion
            Of adoration.

Sure thou wilt joy, by gaining me
    To flie home like a laden bee
        Unto that hive of beams
            And garland-streams.

Virtue

SWEET DAY, so cool, so calm, so bright,
The bridal of the earth and sky,
The dew shall weep thy fall tonight;
              For thou must die.

Sweet rose, whose hue angry and brave
Bids the rash gazer wipe his eye,
Thy root is ever in its grave,
              And thou must die.

Sweet spring, full of sweet days and roses,
A box where sweets compacted lie,
My music shows ye have your closes,
              And all must die.

Only a sweet and virtuous soul,
Like season'd timber, never gives;
But though the whole world turn to coal,
              Then chiefly lives.

Love

LOVE BADE me welcome; yet my soul drew back,
    Guilty of dust and sin.
But quick-ey'd Love, observing me grow slack
    From my first entrance in,
Drew nearer to me, sweetly questioning
    If I lack'd any thing.

'A guest', I answer'd, 'worthy to be here.'
    Love said, 'You shall be he.'
'I the unkind, ungrateful? Ah my dear,
    I cannot look on thee.'
Love took my hand, and smiling did reply,
    'Who made the eyes but I?'

'Truth lord, but I have marr'd them; let my shame
    Go where it doth deserve.'
'And know you not', says Love, 'who bore the blame?'
    'My dear, then I will serve.'
'You must sit down,' says Love, 'and taste my meat.'
    So I did sit and eat.

The Glance

WHEN FIRST thy sweet and gracious eye
Vouchsafed ev'n in the midst of youth and night
To look upon me, who before did lie
           Welt'ring in sin;
  I felt a sugared strange delight,
Passing all cordials made by any art,
Bedew, embalm, and overrun my heart,
           And take it in.

  Since that time many a bitter storm
My soul hath felt, ev'n able to destroy,
Had the malicious and ill-meaning harm
           His swing and way:
  But still thy sweet original joy,
Sprung from thine eye, did work within my soul,
And surging griefs,, when they grew bold, control,
           And got the day.

  If thy first glance so powerful be,
A mirth but opened and sealed up again;
What wonder shall we feel, when we shall see
           Thy full-eyed love!
  When thou shalt look us out of pain,
And one aspect of thine spend in delight
More than a thousand suns disburse in light,
           In heav'n above.

The Flower

HOW FRESH, O Lord, how sweet and clean
Are thy returns! even as the flowers in spring,
    To which, besides their own demean,
The late-past frosts tributes of pleasure bring;
                Grief melts away
                Like snows in May,
    As if there were no such cold thing.

    Who could have thought my shrivelled heart
Could have recovered greenness? It was gone
    Quite underground; as flowers depart
To see their mother-root, when they have blown;
                Where they together
                All the hard weather,
    Dead to the world, keep house unknown.

    These are thy wonders, Lord of power,
Killing and quickening, bringing down to hell
    And up to heaven in an hour;
Making a chiming of a passing-bell.
                We say amiss
                This or that is;
    Thy word is all, if we could spell.

    O that I once past changing were,

Fast in thy Paradise, where no flower can wither!
    Many a spring I shoot up fair,
Offering at heaven, growing and groaning thither;
          Nor doth my flower
          Want a spring shower,
    My sins and I joining together.

    But while I grow in a straight line,
Still upwards bent, as if heaven were mine own,
    Thy anger comes, and I decline;
What frost to that? what pole is not the zone
          Where all things burn,
          When thou dost turn,
    And the least frown of thine is shown?

    And now in age I bud again,
After so many deaths I live and write;
    I once more smell the dew and rain,
And relish versing. O, my only light,
          It cannot be
          That I am he
    On whom thy tempests fell all night.

    These are thy wonders, Lord of love,
To make us see we are but flowers that glide;
    Which when we once can find and prove,
Thou hast a garden for us, where to bide.
          Who would be more,

Swelling through store,
Forfeit their Paradise by their pride.

Easter-Wings

LORD, WHO createst man in
    wealth and store,
Though foolishly he lost
        the same,
Decaying more and more,
        Til he became
        Most poore:
        With thee
        O let me rise
As larks, harmoniously,
    And sing this day thy
        victories:
Then shall the fall further
    the flight in me.

My tender age in sorrow
        did beginne:
And still with sicknesses
        and shame
    Thou didst so punish
        sinne,
        That I became
        Most thinne,
        With thee
        Let me combine

And feel this day thy
victorie:
For, if I imp my wing on
thine,
Affliction shall advance
the flight in me.

Paradise

I BLESS thee, Lord, because I   GROW
Among thy trees, which in a   ROW
To thee both fruit and order   OW.
    What open force, or hidden   CHARM
Can blast my fruit, or bring me   HARM,
While the enclosure is thine   ARM?

Enclose me still for fear I   START.
Be to me rather sharp and   TART,
Than let me want thy hand and   ART.

When thou dost greater judgements   SPARE,
And with thy knife but prune and   PARE,
Ev'n fruitful trees more fruitful   ARE.

Such sharpness shows the sweetest   FREND:
Such cuttings rather heal than   REND:
And such beginnings touch their   END.

The Collar

I STRUCK the board, and cry'd, No more.
I will abroad.
What? shall I ever sigh and pine?
My lines and life are free; free as the rode,
Loose as the winde, as large as store.
Shall I be still in suit?
Have I no harvest but a thorn
To let me bloud, and not restore
What I have lost with cordiall fruit?
Sure there was wine
Before my sighs did drie it: there was corn
Before my tears did drown it.
Is the yeare onely lost to me?
Have I no bayes to crown it?
No flowers, no garlands gay? all blasted?
All wasted?
Not so, my heart: but there is fruit,
And thou hast hands.
Recover all thy sigh-blown age
On double pleasures: leave thy cold dispute
Of what is fit and not. Forsake thy cage,
Thy rope of sands,
Which pettie thoughts have made, and made to thee
Good cable, to enforce and draw,
And be thy law,

While thou didst wink and wouldst not see.
Away; take heed:
I will abroad.
Call in thy deaths head there: tie up thy fears.
He that forbears
To suit and serve his need,
Deserves his load.
But as I rav'd and grew more fierce and wilde
At every word,
Me thoughts I heard one calling, Child!
And I reply'd, My Lord.

SIR WILLIAM DAVENANT
(1606-1668)

To the Queen, Entertained at Night By the Countess of Anglesey

FAIR AS unshaded light, or as the day
In its first birth, when all the year was May;
Sweet as the altar's smoke, or as the new
Unfolded bud, swelled by the early dew:
Smooth as the face of waters first appeared,
Ere tides began to strive, or winds were heard;
Kind as the willing saints, and calmer far
Than in their sleeps forgiven hermits are:
You that are more than our discreeter fear
Dares praise, with such dull art, what make you here?
Here, where the summer is so little seen
That leaves (her cheapest wealth) scarce reach at green,
You come, as if the silver planet were
Misled awhile from her much injured sphere,
And to ease the travails of her beams tonight
In this small lanthorn would contract her light.

SIDNEY GODOLPHIN
(1610-1643)

Song

OR LOVE me less, or love more
 And play not with my liberty;
Either take all, or all restore;
 Bind me at least, or set me free;
Let me some nobler torture find
 Than of a doubtful wavering mind:
Take all my peace; but you betray
 Mine honour too this cruel way.

'Tis true that I have nursed before
 That hope of which I now complain,
And, having little, sought no more,
 Fearing to meet with your disdain:
The sparks of favour you did give,
 I gently blew to make them live;
And yet have gained by all this care
 No rest in hope, nor in despair.

I see you wear that pitying smile

Which you have still vouchsafed my smart,
Content thus cheaply to beguile
    And entertain a harmless heart;
But I no longer can give way
    To hope, which doth so little pay,
And yet I dare no freedom owe
    Whilst you are kind, though but in show.

Then give me more, or give me less,
    Do not disdain a mutual sense,
Or your unpitying beauties dress
    In their own free indifference.
But show not a severer eye,
    Sooner to give me liberty;
For I shall love the very scorn
    Which for my sake you do put on.

RICHARD CRASHAW

(1613?-1649)

To the Countess, Persuading Her
to Resolution in Religion

WHAT HEAVEN-INTREATED HEART is This
Stands trembling at the gate of blisse:
Holds fast the door, yet dares not venture
Fairly to open it, and enter,
Whose DEFINITION is a Doubt
Twixt Life & Death, twixt In & Out.
Say, lingering fair! why comes the birth
Of your brave soul so slowly forth?
Plead your pretences (o you strong
In weakness!) why you choose so long
In labour of yourself to ly,
No daring quite to live nor dy?
Ah linger not, lov'd soul! No,
Who grant at last, a long time tryd
And did his best to have deny'd.
What magick bolt, what mystick Barres
Maintain the will in these strange warres!
What fatal, yet fantastick, bands

Keep Thee free Heart from it's own hands!
So when the year takes cold, we see
Poor waters their own prisoners be.
Fetter'd, & lockt up fast they ly
In a sad self-captivity.
The' astonisht nymphs their flood's strange fate deplore,
To see themselves their on severer shore.
Thou that alone canst thaw this cold,
And fetch the heart from it's strong Hold;
Almighty LOVE! end this long war,
And of a meteor make a star.
O fix this fair INDEFINITE.
And 'mongst thy shafts of soveraign light
Choose out that sure decisive dart
Which has the Key of this close heart,
Knows all the corners of 't, & can control
The self-shut cabinet of an unsearcht soul.
O let it be at last, love's hour.
Raise this tall Trophee of thy Powre;
Come once the conquering way; not to confute
But kill this rebel-word, IRRESOLUTE
That so, inspite of all this peevish strength
Of weakness, she may write REVOL'D AT LENGTH,
Unfold at length, unfold fair flowre
And use the season of love's showre,
Meet his well-meaning Wounds, wiseheart!
And hast to drink the wholesome dart.
That healing shaft, which heaven till now

Hath in love's quiver hid for you.
O Dart of love! arrow of light!
O happy you, if it hit right,
It must not fall in vain, it must
Not mark the dry regardless dust.
Fair one, it is your fate; and brings
Eternal worlds upon its wings.
Meet it with wide-spread arms; and see
Its seat your soul's just centre be.
Disabled dull feares; give faith the day.
To save your life, kill your delay
It is love's siege; and sure to be
Your triumph, though his victory.
'Tis cowardice that keeps this field
And want of courage not to yield.
Yield then, O yield, that love may win
The Fort at last, and let life in.
Yield quickly. Lest perhaps you prove
Death's prey, before the prize of love.
This Fort of your fair selfe, if it be not won,
He is repulst indeed; But you are undone.

from *Hymn of the Nativity*

WELCOME ALL wonders in one sight!
Æternity shut in a span.
Sommer in Winter, Day in Night.
Heaven in earth, and GOD in MAN.
Great little one! whose all-embracing birth
Lifts earth to heaven, stoopes heav'n to earth.

WELCOME! Though not to gold nor silk,
To more than Cæsar's birth right is;
Two sister-seas of Virgin-Milk,
With many a rarely-temper'd kisse
That breathes at once both MAID and MOTHER,
Warmes in the one, cooles in the other.

WELCOME! though not to those gay flyes
Gilded with' Beames of earthly kings;
Slippery soules in smiling eyes;
But to poor Shepherds, home-spun things:
Whose Wealth's their flock; whose wit, to be
Well read in their simplicity.

Yet when young April's husband showers
Shall blesse the fruitfull Maia's bed,
We'll bring the First-born of her flowers
To kisse thy FEET and crown thy HEAD.

To thee, dread Lamb! whose love must keep
The shepheards, more than they the sheep.

TO THEE, meek Majesty! soft KING
Of simple GRACES and sweet LOVES.
Each of us his lamb will bring
Each his pair of sylver Doves;
Till burnt at last in fire of Thy fair eyes,
Our selves become our own best Sacrifice.

JOHN CLEVELAND
(1613-1658)

The Antiplatonick

FOR SHAME, thou everlasting Wooer,
Still saying grace, and never falling to her!
Love that's in contemplation plac't,
Is *Venus* drawn but to the wast.
Unlease your flame confess its gender,
And your Parley cause surrender
Y'are Salamanders of a cold desire
That live untoucht amid the hottest fire.

What though she be a Dame of stone
The Widow of *Pigmalion*;
As hard and unrelenting she,
As the new-crusted *Niobe*;
Or what doth more of statue carry,
A Nunne of the Platonick Quarry!
Love melts the rigour which the rocks have bred,
A flint will break upon a Father-bed.

For you pretty Female Elves

Cease for the candy up yourselves:
No more, you sectaries of the Game,
No more of your calcining flame.
Women commence by *Cupid's* Dart
As a King hunting dubs a Hart,
Love's votaries enthrall each other's soul,
Till both of them live but upon Parole.

Virtue's no more in Woman-kind
But the green sickness of the mind.
Philosophy, their new delight,
A kind of Charcoal appetite.
There's no Sophistry prevails
Where all-convincing love assails;
But the disputing petticoat will warp
As skilfull gamesters are to seeke at harp.

The soldier, that man of iron,
Whom ribs of *horror* all inviron;
That's strung with Wire, instead of Veins,
In those embraces you're in chains,.
Let a Magnetick girl appear,
Straight he turns *Cupid's* Cuirasseer,
Love storms his lips, and takes the Fortress in,
For all the Bristled Turnpikes of his chin.

Since Love's Artillery then checks
The brest-works of the firmest sex,

Come let using affections riot,
Th' are sickly pleases keep a Diet:
Give me a lover bold and free,
Not Eunucht with formality;
Like an Embassador that beds a Queen
With the nice Caution of a sword between.

ABRAHAM COWLEY
(1618-1667)

The Grasshopper

HAPPY INSECT, what can be
In happiness compared to thee?
Fed with nourishment divine,
The dewy morning's gentle wine!
Nature waits upon thee still,
And thy verdant cup does fill;
'Tis filled wherever thou dost tread,
Nature self's thy Ganymede.
Thou dost drink and dance and sing,
Happier than the happiest king!
All the fields which thou dost see,
All the plants, belong to thee;
All that summer hours produce,
Fertile made with early juice.
Man for thee does sow and plough;
Farmer he, and landlord thou!
Thou dost innocently joy,
Nor does thy luxury destroy;
The shepherd gladly heareth thee,

More harmonious than he.

The country hinds with gladness hear,
Prophet of the ripened year!
Thee Phoebus loves, and does inspire;
Phoebus is himself thy sire.
To thee of all things upon Earth,
Life is no longer than thy mirth.
Happy insect, happy thou,
Dost neither age nor winter know.
But when thou'st drunk and danced and sung
Thy fill the flowery leaves among
(Voluptuous and wise withal,
Epicurean animal!),
Sated with thy summer feast,
Thou retir'st to endless rest.

RICHARD LOVELACE
(1618-1656/7)

To Althea, From Prison

WHEN LOVE with unconfined wings
    Hovers within my Gates;
And my divine *Althea* brings
    To whisper at the Grates:
When I lie tangled in her haire,
    And fettered to her eye;
The *Gods* that wanton in the Aire,
    Know no such Liberty.

When flowing Cups run swiftly round
    With no allaying *Thames*,
Our careless heads with Roses bound,
    Our hearts with Loyal Flames;
When thirsty grief in Wine we steepe,
    When Healths and draughts go free,
Fishes that tipple in the Deepe,
    Know no such Liberty.

When (like committed Linnets) I

With shriller throat shall sing
The sweetness, Mercy, Majesty,
    And glories of my KING;
When I shall voice aloud, how Good
    He is, how Great should be;
Inlarged Winds that curle the Flood,
    Know no such Liberty.

Stone Walls do not a Prison make,
    Nor Iron bars a Cage;
Minds innocent and quiet take
    That for an Hermitage;
If I have freedome in my Love,
    And in my soule am free;
Angels alone that sore above
    Injoy such Liberty.

Song: The Scrutiny

WHY SHOULD you swear I am forsworn,
    Since thine I vowed to be?
Lady, it is already morn,
    And 'twas last night I swore to thee
That fond impossibility.

Have I not loved thee much and long,
    A tedious twelve hours' space?
I must all other beauties wrong,
    And rob thee of a new embrace,
Could I still dote upon thy face.

Not but all joy I thy brown hair
    By others may be found;
But I must search the black and fair
    Like skilful mineralists that sound
For treasure in unploughed-up ground.

Then if, when I have loved my round,
    Thou prov'st the pleasant she,
With spoils of meaner beauties crowned
    I laden will return to thee,
Even sated with variety.

ANDREW MARVELL
(1621-1678)

The Definition of Love

MY LOVE is of a birth as rare
As 'tis for object strange and high:
It was begotten by despair
Upon Impossibility.

Magnanimous Despair alone
Could show me so divine a thing,
Where feeble Hope could ne'er have flown
But vainly flappt its Tinsel Wing.

And yet I quickly might arrive
Where my extended Soul is fixt,
But Fate does Iron wedges drive,
And alwaies crouds itself betwixt.

For Fate with jealous Eye does see
Two perfect Loves; nor lets them close:
Their union would her ruin be,
And her Tyrannick pow'r depose.

And therefore her Decrees of Steel
Us as the distant Poles have plac'd,
(Though Loves whole World on us doth wheel)
Not by themselves to be embrac'd.

Unless the giddy Heaven fall,
And Earth some new Convulsion tear;
And, us to join, the World should all
Be cramp'd into a *Planisphere*.

As Lines so Loves *oblige* may well
Themselves in every Angle greet:
But ours so truly *Parallel*,
Though infinite can never meet.

Therefore the Love which us doth bind,
But Fate so enviously debars,
Is the Conjunction of the Mind,
And Opposition of the Stars.

The Coronet

WHEN FOR the thorns with which I long, too long,
    With many a piercing wound,
    My Saviour's head have crown'd,
I seek with garlands to redress that wrong:
    Through every Garden, every Mead,
I gather flow'rs (my fruits are only flow'rs)
    Dismantling all the fragrant Towers
That once adorned my Shepherdesses head.
And now when I have summ'd up all my store,
    Thinking (so I my self deceive)
    So rich a Chaplet thence to weave
As never yet the king of Glory wore:
    Alas I find the Serpent old
    That, twining in his speckled breast,
    About the flow'rs disguis'd does fold,
    With wreaths of Fame and Interest.
Ah, foolish Man, that would'st debase with them,
And mortal Glory, Heaven's Diadem!
But thou who only could'st the Serpent tame,
Either his slipp'ry knots at once untie,
And disintangle all his winding Snare:
Or shatter too with him my curious frame:
And let these wither, so that he may die,
Though set with Skill and chosen out with Care.
That they, while Thou on both their Spoils dost tread,
May crown thy Feet, that could not crown thy Head.

On a Drop of Dew

SEE HOW the Orient Dew,
Shed from the Bosom of the Morn
Into the blowing Roses,
Yet careless of its Mansion new,
For the clear Region where 'twas born,
Round in its self incloses,
And in its little Globes Extent,
Frames as it can its native Element.
How it the purple flow'r does slight,
Scarce touching where it lies,
But gazing back upon the Skies,
Shines with a mournful Light;
Like its own Tear,
Because so long divided from the Sphear.
Restless it roules and unsecure,
Trembling lest it grow impure:
Till the warm Sun pity it's Pain,
And to the Skies exhale it back again.
So the Soul, that Drop, that Ray
Of the clear Fountain of Eternal Day,
Could it within the humane flow'r be seen,
Remembering still its former height,
Shuns the sweet leaves and blossoms green;
And, recollecting its own Light,
Does, in its pure and circling thoughts, express

The greater heaven in an Heaven less.
   In how coy a figure wound,
   Every way it turns away:
   So the World excluding round,
   Yet receiving in the Day.
   Dark beneath, but bright above:
   Here disdaining, there in Love,
 How loose an easie hence to go:
 How girt and ready to ascend.
 Moving but on a point below,
 It all about does upwards bend.
Such did the Manna's sacred Dew destil;
White, and intire, though congeal'd and chill.
Congeal'd on Earth: but does, dissolving, run
Into the Glories of th' Almighty Sun.

The Garden

HOW VAINLY men themselves amaze
To win the palm, the oak, or bays;
And their uncessant labours see
Crowned from some single herb or tree,
Whose short and narrow verged shade
Does prudently their toils upbraid;
While all flowers and all trees do close
To weave the garlands of repose.

Fair Quiet, have I found thee here,
And Innocence, thy sister dear!
Mistaken long, I sought you then
In busy companies of men,
Your sacred plant, if here below,
Only among the plants will grow.
Society is all but rude,
To this delicious solitude.

No white nor red was ever seen
So am'rous as this lovely green.
Fond lovers, cruel as their flame,
Cut in these trees their mistress's name.
Little, alas, they know, or heed,
How far these beauties hers exceed!
Fair trees! wheres'e'er your barks I wound,

No name shall but your own be found.

When we have run our passion's heat,
Love hither makes his best retreat.
The gods, that mortal beauty chase,
Still in a tree did end their race.
Apollo hunted Daphne so,
Only that she might laurel grow.
And Pan did after Syrinx speed,
Not as a nymph, but for a reed.

What wondrous life in this I lead!
Ripe apples drop about my head;
The luscious clusters of the vine
Upon my mouth do crush their wine;
The nectarine, and curious peach,
Into my hands themselves do reach;
Stumbling on melons, as I pass,
Ensnared with flowers I fall on grass.

Meanwhile the mind, from pleasures less,
Withdraws into its happiness:
The mind, that ocean where each kind
Does straight its own resemblance find;
Yet it creates, transcending these,
Far other worlds, and other seas;
Annihilating all that's made
To a green thought in a green shade.

Here at the fountain's sliding foot,
Or at some fruit-tree's mossy root,
Casting the body's vest aside,
My soul into the boughs does glide:
There like a bird it sits, and sings,
Then whets, and combs its silver wings;
And, till prepared for longer flight,
Waves in its plumes the various light.

Such was that happy garden-state,
While man there walked without a mate:
After a place so pure, and sweet,
What other help could yet be meet!
But 'twas beyond a mortal's share
To wander solitary there:
Two paradises 'twere in one
To live in paradise alone.

How well the skilful gardener drew
Of flowers and herbs this dial new;
Where from above the milder sun
Does through a fragrant zodiac run;
And, as it works, th' industrious bee
Computes its time as well as we,
How could such sweet and wholesome hours
Be reckoned but with herbs and flowers!

HENRY VAUGHAN
(1621-1695)

'They are all gone into the world of light!'

THEY ARE all gone into the world of light!
    And I alone sit ling'ring here;
Their very memory is fair and bright,
        And my sad thoughts doth clear.

It glows and glitters in my cloudy breast
    Like stars upon some gloomy grove,
Or those faint beams in which this hill is dressed,
    After the sun's remove.

I see them walking in an air of glory,
    Whose light doth trample on my days:
My days, which are at best but dull and hoary,
        Mere glimmering and decays.

O holy hope! and high humility,
    High as the heavens above!
These are your walks, and you have showed them me
        To kindle my cold love,

Dear, beauteous death! the jewel of the just,
  Shining nowhere, but in the dark;
What mysteries do lie beyond thy dust;
    Could man outlook that mark!

He that hath found some fledged bird's nest, may know
  At first sight, if the bird be flown;
But what fair well, or grove he sings in now,
    That is to him unknown.

And yet, as Angels in some brighter dreams
  Call to the soul, when man doth sleep:
So some strange thoughts transcend our wonted themes,
    And into glory peep.

If a star were confined into a tomb
  Her captive flames must needs burn there;
But when the hand that locked her up, gives room
    She'll shine through all the sphere.

O Father of eternal life, and all
  Created glories under thee!
Resume thy spirit from this world of thrall
    Into true liberty.

Either disperse these mists, which blot and fill
  My perspective (still) as they pass,

Or else remove me hence unto that hill,
Where I shall need no glass.

The Retreat

HAPPY THOSE early days! when I
Shined in my Angel-infancy.
Before I understood this place
Appointed for my second race,
Or taught my soul to fancy aught
But a white, celestial thought,
When yet I had not walked above
A mile, or two, from my first love,
And looking back (at that short space,)
Could see a glimpse of his bright-face;
When on some *gilded cloud*, or *flower*
My gazing souls would dwell an hour,
And in those weaker glories spy
Some shadows of eternity;
Before I taught my tongue to wound
My conscience with a sinful sound,
Or had the black art to dispense
A several sin to every sense,
But felt through all this fleshly dress
Bright *shoots* of everlastingness.
　　O how I long to travel back
And tread against that ancient track!
That I might once more reach that plain,
Where first I left my glorious train,
From whence the enlightened spirits sees

That shady city of palm trees;
But (ah!) my soul with too much stay
Is drunk, and staggers in the way.
Some men a forward motion love,
But I by backward steps would move,
And when this dust falls to the urn
In that state I came return.

The World

1

I SAW Eternity the other night
Like a great *Ring* of pure and endless light,
        All calm, as it was bright,
And round beneath it, Time in hours, days, years
        Driven by the spheres
Like a vast shadow moved, in which the world
        And all her train were hurled;
The doting lover in his quaintest straining
        Did there complain,
Near him, his lute, his fancy, and his flights,
        Wit's sour delights,
With gloves, and knots the silly snares of pleasure
        Yet his dear treasure
All scattered lay, while he his eyes did pour
        Upon a flower.

2

The darksome states-man hung with weights and woe
Like a thick midnight-fog moved there so slow
        He did nor stay, nor go;
Condemning thoughts (like sad eclipses) scowl
        Upon his soul,

And clouds of crying witnesses without
        Pursued him with one shout.
Yet digged the mole, and lest his ways be found
        Worked under ground,
Where he did clutch his prey, but one did see
        That policy,
Churches and altars fed him, perjuries
        Were gnats and flies,
It rained about him blood and tears, but he
        Drank them as free.

3

The fearful miser on a heap of rust
Sat pining all his life there, did scarce trust
        His own hands with the dust,
Yet would not place one piece above, but lives
        In fear of thieves.
Thousands there were as frantic as himself
        And hugged each one his pelf,
The down-right epicure placed heaven in sense
        And scorned pretence
While others slipped into a wide excess
        Said little less;
The weaker sort slight, trivial wares enslave
        Who think them brave,
And poor, despised truth sat counting by
        Their victory.

4

Yet some, who all this while did weep and sing,
And sing, and weep, soared up into the *Ring*,
      But most would use no wing.
O fools (said I,) thus to prefer dark night
      Before true light,
To live in grots, and caves, and hate the day
      Because it shows the way,
The way which from this dead and dark abode
      Leads up to God,
A way where you might tread the sun, and he
      More bright than he.
But as I did their madness so discuss
      One whispered thus,
This ring the bride-groom did for none provide
      But for his bride.

The Morning-Watch

O JOYS! infinite sweetness! with what flowers,
And shoots of glory, my soul breaks, and buds!
          All the long hours
          Of night, and rest
          Through the still shrouds
          Of sleep, and clouds,
     This dew fell on my breast;
          Of how it *blows*,
And *spirits* all my earth! hark! In what rings,
And *hymning circulations* the quick world
          Awakes, and sings;
          The rising winds,
          And falling springs,
          Birds, beasts, all things
     Adore him in their kinds.
          Thus all is hurled
In sacred *hymns*, and *order*, the great *chime*
And *symphony* of nature. Prayer is
          The world in tune,
          A spirit-voice,
          And vocal joys
     Whose *echo is* heaven's bliss.
          O let me climb
When I lie down! The pious soul by night
Is like a clouded star, whose beams though said

To shed their light
Under some cloud
    Yet are above,
    And shine, and move
Beyond that misty shroud.
    So in my bed
That curtained grave, though sleep, like ashes, hide
My lamp, and life, both shall in thee abide.

Peace

MY SOUL, there is a country
    Far beyond the stars,
Where stands a winged sentry
    All skillful in the wars,
There above noise, and danger
    Sweet peace sits crowned with smiles,
And one born in a manger
    Commands the beauteous files,
He is thy gracious friend,
    And (O my soul awake!)
Did in pure love descend
    To die here for thy sake,
If thou canst get but thither,
    There grows the flower of peace,
The rose that cannot wither,
    Thy fortress, and thy ease;
Leave then thy foolish ranges;
    For none can thee secure,
But one, who never changes,
    Thy God, thy life, thy cure.

The Night

THROUGH THAT pure *Virgin-shrine,*
That sacred veil drawn o'er thy glorious noon
That men might look and live as glow-worms shine,
      And face the moon:
    Wise *Nicodemus* saw such light
    As made him know his God by night.

     Most blest believer he!
Who in that land of darkness and blind eyes
Thy long expected healing wings could see,
      When thou didst rise,
    And what can nevermore be done,
    Did at mid-night speak with the Sun!

     O who will tell me, where
He found thee at that dead and silent hour!
What hallowed solitary ground did bear
      So rare a flower,
    Within whose sacred leaves did lie
    The fullness of the Deity.

     No mercy-seat of gold,
No dead and dusty *Cherub*, nor carved stone,
But his own living works did my Lord hold
      And lodge alone;

Where *trees* and *herbs* did watch and peep
And wounds, while the *Jews* did sleep.

Dear night! this world's defeat;
The stop to busy fools; care's check and curb;
The day of Spirits; my soul's calm retreat
    Which none disturb!
    Christ's progress, and his prayer time;
    The hours to which high Heaven doth chime.

God's silent, searching flight:
When my Lord's head is filled with dew, and all
His locks are wet with the clear drops of night;
    His still,s oft call;
    His knocking time; the soul's dumb watch,
    When Spirits their fair kindred catch.

Were all my loud, evil days
Calm and unhaunted as is thy dark Tent,
Whose peace but by some *Angel's* wing or voice
    Is seldom rent;
    Then I in Heaven all the long year
    Would keep, and never wander here.

But living where the sun
Doth all things wake, and where all mix and tire
Themselves and others,I consent and run
    To every mire,

And by this world's ill-guiding light,
Err more than I can do by night.

There is in God (some say)
A deep, but dazzling darkness; as men here
Say it is late and dusky, because they
        See not all clear;
  O for that night! where I in him
  Might live invisible and dim.

Midnight

I

WHEN TO my eyes
(Whilst deep sleep others catches,)
Thine host of spies
The stars shine in their watches,
I do survey
Each busy ray,
And how they work, and wind,
And wish each beam
My soul doth stream,
With the like ardour shined;
What emanations,
Quick vibrations
And bright stirs are there?
What thin ejections,
Cold affections,
And slow motions here?

2

Thy heavens (some say,)
Are a fiery-liquid light,
            Which mingling aye
Streams, and flames thus to the sight.
            Come then, my god!
            Shine on this blood,
    And water in one beam,
            And thou shalt see
        Kindled by thee
Both liquors burn, and stream.
            O what bright quickness,
            Active brightness,
    And celestial flows
            Will follow after
            On that water,
Which thy spirit blows!

The Revival

UNFOLD, UNFOLD! take in his light,
Who makes thy cares more short than night.
The joys, which with his *Day-star* rise,
He deals to all, but drowsy eyes:
And what the men of this world miss,
Some *drops* and *dews* of future bliss.
    Hark! how his *winds* have changed their *note*,
And with warm *whispers* cal thee out.
The *frosts are past*, the *storms* are gone:
And backward *life* at last comes on.
The lofty *groves* in express joys
Reply unto the *turtle's* voice,
And here in *dust* and *dirt*, O here
The *lilies* o his love appear!

THOMAS STANLEY
(1625-1678)

The Repulse

NOT THAT by this disdain
      I am releas'd,
And freed from thy tyrannick chain,
    Do I myself think blest;

Not that thy Flame shall burn
      No more; for know
That I shall into ashes turn,
    Before this fire doth go.

Nor yet that unconfin'd
      I now may rove,
And with new beauties please my mind;
    But that thou ne'r didst love:

For since thou hast no part
      Felt of this flame,
I only from thy tyrant heart
    Repuls'd, not banish'd am.

To lose what once was mine
                Would grieve me more
Than those inconstant sweets of thine
    Had pleas'd my soul before.

Now I have lost the bliss
              I ne'r possest
And spright of fate am blest in this,
    That I was never blest.

THOMAS TRAHERNE

(1636?-1674)

Wonder

HOW LIKE an angel came I down!
How bright are all things here!
When first among his works I did appear,
Oh, how their Glory me did crown!
The world resembled his Eternity,
In which my soul did walk;
And every thing that I did see
Did with me talk.

The skies in their magnificence,
The lively, lovely air;
Oh, how divine, how soft, how sweet, how fair!
The stars did entertain my sense,
And all the works of God so bright and pure,
So rich and great did seem
As if they ever must endure
In my esteem.

A native health and innocence

Within my bones did grow,
And while my God did all his glories show,
    I felt a vigour in my sense
That was all spirit. I within did flow
        With seas of life, like wine;
    I nothing in the world did know,
            But 'twas divine.

Harsh, ragged objects were concealed,
      Oppressions, tears, and cries,
Sins, griefs, complaints, dissentions, weeping eyes,
    Were hid: and only things revealed
Which heavenly spirits and the angels prize.
    The State of Innocence
And Bliss, not trades and poverties,
        Did fill my sense.

The streets were paved with golden stones,
    The boys and girls were mine;
Oh, how did all their lovely faces shine!
    The Sons of Men were Holy Ones,
Joy, Beauty, Welfare did appear to me,
      And every thing which here I found,
    While like an angel I did see,
        Adorned the ground.

Rich diamond, and pearl, and gold
    In every place was seen;

Rare splendours, yellow, blue, red, white, and green,
    Mine eyes did everywhere behold;
Great Wonders clothed with Glory did appear,
        Amazement was my Bliss.
    That and my wealth was everywhere:
        No Joy to this....

The Rapture

SWEET INFANCY!
O fire of heaven! O sacred light!
    How fair and bright!
    How great am I,
Whom all the world doth magnify!

    O heavenly joy!
O great and sacred blessedness,
    Which I possess!
    So great a joy
Who did into my arms convey?

    From god above
Being sent, the heavens me enflame
    To praise his name.
    The stars do move!
The burning sun doth show his love.

    Oh how divine
Am I! To all this sacred wealth,
    This life and health,
    Who raised? Who mine
Did make the same? What hand divine?

from *My Spirit*

O JOY! O wonder and delight!
  O sacred mystery!
My Soul a Spirit infinite!
An image of the Deity!
  A pure substantial light!
That Being greatest which doth nothing seem!
Why, 'twas my all, I nothing did esteem
But that alone. A strange mysterious sphere!
   A deep abyss
   That sees and is
The only proper place of Heavenly Bliss.
  To its Creator 'tis so near
    In love and excellence,
     In life and sense,
In greatness, worth, and nature; and so dear,
   In it, without hyperbole,
   The Son and friend of God we see.

  A strange extended orb of Joy,
    Proceeding from within,
  Which did on every side, convey
  Itself, and being nigh of kin
    To Go did every way
Dilate itself even in an instant, and
Like an indivisible centre stand,

At once surrounding all eternity.
         'Twas not a sphere,
         Yet did appear,
One infinite. 'Twas somewhat every where,
         And though it had a power to see
              Far more, yet still it shin'd
                   And was a mind
Exerted, for it saw Infinity.
         'Twas not a sphere, but 'twas a might
         Invisible, and yet gave light.

         O wondrous Self! O sphere of light,
              O sphere of joy most fair
         O act, O power infinite;
         O subtile and unbounded air!
              O living or of sight!
Thou which within me art, yet me! Thou eye,
And temple of His whole infinity!
         O what a world art Thou! A world within!
              All things appear,
              All objects are
Alive in Thee! Supersubstantial, rare,
         Above themselves, and nigh of kin
              To those pure things we find
                   In His great mind
Who made the world! Tho' now eclipsed by sin
         There they are useful and divine,
         Exalted there they ought to shine.

Love

    O NECTAR! O delicious stream!
O ravishing and only pleasure! Where
        Shall such another theme
Inspire my tongue with joy or please mine ear!
      Abridgement of delights!
        And Queen of sights!
O mine of rarities! O Kingdom wide!
O more! O cause of all! O glorious Bride!
   O God! O Bride of God! O King!
   O soul and crown of everything!

    Did not I covet to behold
Some endless monarch, that did always live
      In palaces of gold,
Willing all kingdoms, realms, and crowns to give
      Unto my soul! Whose love
       A spring might prove
Of endless glories, honours, friendships, pleasures,
Joys, praises, beauties and celestial treasures!
   Lo, now I see there's such a King,
   The fountain-head of everything!

    Did my ambition ever dream
Of such a Lord, of such a love! Did I
      Expect so sweet a stream

As this at any time! Could any eye
        Believe it? Why all power
            Is used here;
Joys down from Heaven on my head do shower,
And Jove beyond the fiction doth appear
    Once more in golden rain to come
    To Danæ's pleasing fruitful womb.
    His Ganymede! His life! His joy!
Or He comes down to me, or takes me up
        That I might be His boy,
And fill, and taste, and give, and drink the cup.
        But those (tho' great) are all
            Too short and small,
Too weak and feeble pictures to express
The true mysterious depths of Blessedness.
    I am His image, and His friend,
    His son, bride, glory, temple, end.

Shadows in the Water

IN UNEXPERIENCED infancy
Many a sweet mistake doth lie:
Mistake though false, intending true;
A seeming somewhat more than view;
That doth instruct the mind
In things that lie behind,
And many secrets to us show
Which afterwards we come to know.

Thus did I by the water's brink
Another world beneath me think;
And while the lofty spacious skies
Reversèd there, abused mine eyes,
I fancied other feet
Came mine to touch or meet;
As by some puddle I did play
Another world within it lay.

Beneath the water people drowned,
Yet with another heaven crowned,
In spacious regions seemed to go
As freely moving to and fro:
In bright and open space
I saw their very face;
Eyes, hands, and feet they had like mine;

Another sun did with them shine.

'Twas strange that people there should walk,
And yet I could not hear them talk:
That through a little watery chink,
Which one dry ox or horse might drink,
We other worlds should see,
Yet not admitted be;
And other confines there behold
Of light and darkness, heat and cold.

I called them oft, but called in vain;
No speeches we could entertain:
Yet did I there expect to find
Some other world, to please my mind.
I plainly saw by these
A new antipodes,
Whom, though they were so plainly seen,
A film kept off that stood between.

By walking men's reversèd feet
I chanced another world to meet;
Though it did not to view exceed
A phantom, 'tis a world indeed;
Where skies beneath us shine,
And earth by art divine
Another face presents below,
Where people's feet against ours go.

Within the regions of the air,
Compassed about with heavens fair,
Great tracts of land there may be found
Enriched with fields and fertile ground;
Where many numerous hosts
In those far distant coasts,
For other great and glorious ends
Inhabit, my yet unknown friends.

O ye that stand upon the brink,
Whom I so near me through the chink
With wonder see: what faces there,
Whose feet, whose bodies, do ye wear?
I my companions see
In you another me.
They seemèd others, but are we;
Our second selves these shadows be.

Look how far off those lower skies
Extend themselves! scarce with mine eyes
I can them reach. O ye my friends,
What secret borders on those ends?
Are lofty heavens hurled
'Bout your inferior world?
Are yet the representatives
Of other peoples' distant lives?

Of all the playmates which I knew
That here I do the image view
In other selves, what can it mean?
But that below the purling stream
Some unknown joys there be
Laid up in store for me;
To which I shall, when that thin skin
Is broken, be admitted in.

GALLERY OF POETS

John Donne

Robert Herrick

George Herbert, 1674

Andrew Marvell, c, 1655-60

Henry Vaughan

A Note On Metaphysical Poetry

A list of poets classed as 'Metaphysical' by a critic includes:

Thomas Carew (1594/5-1640),
William Cartwright (1611-1643),
John Cleveland (1613-1658),
Abraham Cowley (1618-1667),
Richard Crashaw (1612-1649),
William Davenant (1606-1668),
John Donne (1572-1631),
Richard Fanshawe (1608-1666),
Owen Feltham (1602?-1668),
Sidney Godolphin (1610-1643),
Fulke Greville (1554-1628),
William Habington (1605-1654),
John Hall (1627-1656),

George Herbert (1593-1633),
Robert Herrick (1591-1674),
Ben Jonson (1572?-1637),
Henry King (1592-1669),
Francis Kynaston (1587-1642),
Richard Lovelace (1618-1656/7),
Andrew Marvell (1621-1678),
Francis Quarles (1592-1644),
Walter Raleigh (*c*.1552-1618),
John Suckling (1609-1642),
Aurealian Townshend (*c*.1583-*c*. 1651),
Thomas Traherne (1637/8-1674),
Henry Vaughan (1621/2-1695)
and Henry Wotton (1568-1639) (in Evans).

In Herbert Grierson's 1921 anthology (*Metaphysical Lyrics and Poems of the Seventeenth Century*) six poets formed the centre of Metaphysical poetry: John Donne (who had 35 poems), George Herbert (13 poems), Henry Vaughan (11), Andrew Marvell (10), Thomas Carew (10) and Richard Crashaw (6). In Helen Gardener's 1957 anthology, Donne had 40 poems, Herbert had 24, Vaughan 17, Marvell 14, Carew 10 and Crashaw 9 poems.

I have included the main Metaphysical poets – no anthology would be complete without Herbert, Vaughan, Traherne, Crashaw, Donne and Marvell. These appear to be (according to most literary critics) the poets central to Metaphysical poetry. Naturally, then, my selection draws from these poets more than the others.

John Donne, universally accepted as the leading light of the Metaphysical poets, is anthologized with poems such as 'The Extasie', 'Air and Angels' and various *Holy Sonnets*. Helen Gardner, in her Metaphysical poetry anthology, uses the following Donne poems, among others: 'The Flea', 'The Canonization', 'Air and Angels', 'Sweetest Love', 'Love's Growth', 'Love's Alchemy', 'The Extasie', 'The Will', 'The Relique', ''The Dream', 'Elegy: On His Mistriss Going to Bed', '*Song:* Go and Catch a Falling Star', *Holy Sonnets:* 'As due by many', 'Oh my black soul', 'This is my play's', 'At the round Earth's imagined corners, blow', 'If poisonous', 'Death be not proud, though some have called thee', 'Batter my heart, three-personed God', 'Since she whom I lov'd hath paid her last debt', 'Good Friday', 'A Hymn to Christ' and 'Hymn to God My God, in My Sickness'.

In the 20th century there was a renewal of interest in the Metaphysical poets. Critics who became instrumental in this renaissance of the Metaphysicals included Johnson, Coleridge, Helen Gardener, F.R. Leavis, Gosse, T.S. Eliot, L.C. Martin, Mario Praz, Louis L. Martz, Rosemond Tuve, Evelyn Simpson, J.B. Leishman, Joan Bennett, F.E. Hutchinson, Pierre Legouis and Herbert J.C. Grierson.[1] Of these, the chief name, among critics or poets, is Eliot. His essays on the Metaphysical poets ensured at least some sort of revival.

Frances Austin writes: 'Uncertainty in all spheres of life conditioned the religious verse written in the first half of the Seventeenth century.' (1) I have concentrated more on the 'religious' or 'divine' poems of the Metaphysical poets. These poems best represent, I think, the Metaphysical poetic stance. In this era of religious uncertainty, many of the poems are full of conviction and passion. Some of the poems, such as those by Vaughan and Traherne in particular, are ecstatic.[2] The emphasis on religion did not mean that the poets of this time were writing in quiet cloisters. John Donne, for example, led a busy life which included sailing in the two adventures to Cadiz and the islands of Essex. Andrew Marvell was an MP, an assistant to Milton, and a social campaigner. Traherne went to London from the country to work at the Court as a chaplain to Sir Orlando Bridgeman, Lord Keeper of the Great Seal. Vaughan worked for years as a doctor. Richard Crashaw lived on the continent (Holland, Paris, Italy). The Court and secular poets – Cowley, Waller, Suckling, Lovelace, Herrick, Davenant, Cleveland – were (usually) Royalists, embroiled in the seventeenth century conflict between State and King.

The 'Metaphysical' poetic style is witty, learned, subjective, sensual, intellectual, reflective, philosophical, baroque, intense, sometimes ecstatic. Metaphysical poetry was passion/ emotion modified by intellect/ wit ('passionate ratiocination' Herbert Grierson called it, while T.S. Eliot described Donne's poetry as experience modified by (his) sensibility. Helen Gardener said

Metaphysical verse was 'an expanded epigram', and Margaret Willy called it 'feeling thought'. Metaphysical poetry used satire and irony as well as the new science (biology, mathematics, cosmology and microcosmic emphasis). It is a poetry concerned with living for the present, with philosophical and religious subjects, with, in short, the soul.[3] It is a dramatic poetry, essentially lyrical, often rough at the edges, with its love of individualized verse forms and writing poems as long as they needed to be. After the adherence to traditional stanzas of Elizabethan poetry (the sonnet being the most obvious type), the Metaphysical poets employed a wide variety of forms and metrical patterns. Thomas Traherne, for example, wrote in a new verse form each time he wrote a poem. Poets such as Vaughan, Traherne and Marvell give the impression of writing until they've finished what they wanted to say. Their poetic forms were open – a short line here, an extended stanza there, as the subject demanded.

Metaphysical poetry was partly 'Classical', partly 'Christian' and 'religious'; it was partly humanist, partly Cavalier and partly Elizabethan. John Donne, for example, was just as much Elizabethan, post-Petrarchan, Renaissance and 'Classical' as 'Metaphysical'.[4] Some critics separate the Metaphysical poets' love poems from their religious ones. The division maybe useful, but it is not how poets write. The boundaries between profane/ sacred, love/ religion, secular/ divine is not that clearly marked by the poets themselves. The 'religious' poems of the Metaphysical poets are often their most erotic. They write of God, the beloved, and their relationship to Him, in erotic terms. In poems such as 'The World', for example, Henry Vaughan narrates the old notion of the soul being mystically married to the Bridegroom (God). These notions of the Christian *hieros gamos* (or 'spiritual marriage') and other fusions of sexual and sacred imagery were at their most vivid in the Spanish and Italian Catholic mystics, such as St Teresa of Avila, St John of the Cross, Juan de Los Angeles, Ignatius Loyola and Miguel de Molinos. The imagery of Catholic mystical sensuality is at its most pronounced in the most obviously and flamboyantly erotic of the Metaphysical poets, Richard Crashaw. His poems are full of erotic fluids. Crashaw is associated with extravagant and 'baroque' artists such as Marino, Bernin and St Teresa.[5] Metaphysical poetry would probably not be as popular as it is today without it engaging sensuality and emotion in such a lyrical and lucid way.

Notes

1. See Hammond, 27-28; Willy, 1.
2. Some critics have compared Vaughan to Donne –
unfavourably, of course. Vaughan (like Herrick) suffers
from being compared to Donne. (Peter Cairns: "The flint
and the world of light: The originality of Henry
Vaughan", in Cookson, 1990, 69) But most of the
Metaphysical poets suffer when compared to Donne, just
as just about all British poets suffer when compared to
Shakespeare. One critic claims that 'Vaughan wrote few
wholly successful poems' (Rogers, 1987, ch. 4), a claim
easily refuted by a glance at Vaughan's *Complete Poems.*
3. See Handley, 1991, 7-8.
4. Trevor James: *The Metaphysical Poets*, Longman,
1988, 30f.
5. See M.F. Bertanesco: *Crashaw and the Baroque*,
Alabama 1971; R.V. Young: *Richard Crashaw and the*

Spanish Golden Age, 1982; L. Martz: *The Light of Love*, 1969; R.T. Petersson: *The Art of Ecstasy*, 1970. On Crashaw as the exuberant, sensual poet of the grandiose European baroque type, see Thomas F. Healy: *Richard Crashaw*, E.J. Brill, Leiden 1986, 1.

Bibliography

Frances Austin: *The Language of the Metaphysical Poets*, Macmillan 1992

Joan Bennet, ed: *Five Metaphysical Poets*, Cambridge University Press 1964

N. Coms, ed: *The Cambridge Companion to English Poetry: Donne to Marvell*, Cambridge University Press 1993

L. Cookson & B. Longhrey, eds: *The Metaphysical Poets*, Longman 1990

Gillian Evans: *The Age of the Metaphysicals*, Blackie, Glasgow 1978

Alastair Fowler, ed: *The New Oxford Book of Seventeenth Century Verse*, Oxford University Press 1991

Helen Gardner, ed: *The Metaphysical Poets*, Oxford University Press 1957/67

Herbet J.C. Grierson, ed: *Metaphysical Lyrics and Poems*

of the Seventeenth Century, Oxford University Press 1921

Graham Handley: *The Metaphysical Poets, Brodie's Notes,* Pan 1991

Gerald Hammond, ed: *The MetaphySical Poets, A Casebook,* Macmillan 1974

—*Fleeting Things: English Poets and Poems 1616-1660*, Harvard University Press 1990

Leah S. Marcus: *The Politics of Mirth: Jonson, Herrick, Milton, Marvell and the Defense of Old Holiday Pastimes*, University of Chicago Press 1986

P. Rogers: *The Oxford Illustrated History of English Literature*, Oxford University Press 1987

Margaret Willy: *The Metaphysical Poets*, Arnold 1971

ARTS, PAINTING, SCULPTURE

web: www.crmoon.com • e-mail: cresmopub@yahoo.co.uk

The Art of Andy Goldsworthy
Andy Goldsworthy: Touching Nature
Andy Goldsworthy in Close-Up
Andy Goldsworthy: Pocket Guide
Andy Goldsworthy In America
Land Art: A Complete Guide
The Art of Richard Long
Richard Long: Pocket Guide
Land Art In Great Britain
Land Art in Close-Up
Land Art In the U.S.A.
Land Art: Pocket Guide
Installation Art in Close-Up
Minimal Art and Artists In the 1960s and After
Colourfield Painting
Land Art DVD, TV documentary
Andy Goldsworthy DVD, TV documentary
The Erotic Object: Sexuality in Sculpture From Prehistory to the Present Day
Sex in Art: Pornography and Pleasure in Painting and Sculpture
Postwar Art
Sacred Gardens: The Garden in Myth, Religion and Art
Glorification: Religious Abstraction in Renaissance and 20th Century Art
Early Netherlandish Painting
Jasper Johns
Brice MardenLeonardo da Vinci
Piero della Francesca
Giovanni Bellini
Fra Angelico: Art and Religion in the Renaissance
Mark Rothko: The Art of Transcendence
Frank Stella: American Abstract Artist
Alison Wilding: The Embrace of Sculpture
Vincent van Gogh: Visionary Landscapes
Eric Gill: Nuptials of God
Constantin Brancusi: Sculpting the Essence of Things
Max Beckmann
Gustave Moreau
Caravaggio
Egon Schiele: Sex and Death In Purple Stockings
Delizioso Fotografico Fervore: Works In Process I
Sacro Cuore: Works In Process 2
The Light Eternal: J.M.W. Turner
The Madonna Glorified: Karen Arthurs

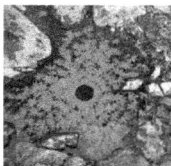

LITERATURE

J.R.R. Tolkien: The Books, The Films, The Whole Cultural Phenomenon
J.R.R. Tolkien: Pocket Guide
Beauties, Beasts and Enchantment: Classic French Fairy Tales
Tolkien's Heroic Quest
Brothers Grimm: German Popular Stories
Sexing Hardy: Thomas Hardy and Feminism
Thomas Hardy's *Tess of the d'Urbervilles*
Thomas Hardy's *Jude the Obscure*
Thomas Hardy: The Tragic Novels
Love and Tragedy: Thomas Hardy
The Poetry of Landscape in Hardy
Wessex Revisited: Thomas Hardy and John Cowper Powys
Wolfgang Iser: Essays and Interviews
Petrarch, Dante and the Troubadours
Maurice Sendak and the Art of Children's Book Illustration
Andrea Dworkin
Cixous, Irigaray, Kristeva: The *Jouissance* of French Feminism
Julia Kristeva: Art, Love, Melancholy, Philosophy, Semiotics and Psychoanalysis
Hélène Cixous I Love You: The *Jouissance* of Writing
Luce Irigaray: Lips, Kissing, and the Politics of Sexual Difference
Peter Redgrove: Here Comes the Flood
Peter Redgrove: Sex-Magic-Poetry-Cornwall
Lawrence Durrell: Between Love and Death, East and West
Love, Culture & Poetry: Lawrence Durrell
Cavafy: Anatomy of a Soul
German Romantic Poetry: Goethe, Novalis, Heine, Hölderlin
Novalis: *Hymns To the Night*
Feminism and Shakespeare
Shakespeare: *The Sonnets*
Shakespeare: Love, Poetry & Magic
The Passion of D.H. Lawrence
D.H. Lawrence: Symbolic Landscapes
D.H. Lawrence: Infinite Sensual Violence
The Ecstasies of John Cowper Powys
Sensualism and Mythology: The Wessex Novels of John Cowper Powys
Amorous Life: John Cowper Powys (H.W. Fawkner)
Postmodern Powys: New Essays on John Cowper Powys (Joe Boulter)
Rethinking Powys: Critical Essays on John Cowper Powys
Paul Bowles & Bernardo Bertolucci
Rainer Maria Rilke
Joseph Conrad: *Heart of Darkness*
In the Dim Void: Samuel Beckett
Samuel Beckett Goes into the Silence
André Gide: Fiction and Fervour
Jackie Collins and the Blockbuster Novel
Blinded By Her Light: The Love-Poetry of Robert Graves

POETRY

Ursula Le Guin: *Walking In Cornwall*
Peter Redgrove: Here Comes The Flood
Peter Redgrove: Sex-Magic-Poetry-Cornwall
Dante: Selections From the *Vita Nuova*
Petrarch, Dante and the Troubadours
William Shakespeare: *The Sonnets*
William Shakespeare: Complete Poems
Blinded By Her Light: The Love-Poetry of Robert Graves
Emily Dickinson: Selected Poems
Emily Brontë: Poems
Thomas Hardy: Selected Poems
Percy Bysshe Shelley: Poems
John Keats: Selected Poems
John Keats: Poems of 1820
D.H. Lawrence: Selected Poems
Edmund Spenser: Poems
Edmund Spenser: *Amoretti*
John Donne: Poems
Henry Vaughan: Poems
Sir Thomas Wyatt: Poems
Robert Herrick: Selected Poems
Rilke: Space, Essence and Angels in the Poetry of Rainer Maria Rilke
Rainer Maria Rilke: Selected Poems
Friedrich Hölderlin: Selected Poems
Arseny Tarkovsky: Selected Poems
Paul Verlaine: Selected Poems
Novalis: *Hymns To the Night*
Arthur Rimbaud: Selected Poems
Arthur Rimbaud: *A Season in Hell*
Arthur Rimbaud and the Magic of Poetry
D.J. Enright: By-Blows
Jeremy Reed: *Brigitte's Blue Heart*
Jeremy Reed: *Claudia Schiffer's Red Shoes*
Gorgeous Little Orpheus
Radiance: New Poems
Crescent Moon Book of Nature Poetry
Crescent Moon Book of Love Poetry
Crescent Moon Book of Mystical Poetry
Crescent Moon Book of Elizabethan Love Poetry
Crescent Moon Book of Metaphysical Poetry
Crescent Moon Book of Romantic Poetry
Pagan America: New American Poetry

MEDIA, CINEMA, FEMINISM and CULTURAL STUDIES

J.R.R. Tolkien: The Books, The Films, The Whole Cultural Phenomenon
J.R.R. Tolkien: Pocket Guide
The *Lord of the Rings* Movies: Pocket Guide
The Ghost Dance: The Origins of Religion
The Cinema of Hayao Miyazaki
Hayao Miyazaki: *Princess Mononoke*: Pocket Movie Guide
Hayao Miyazaki: *Spirited Away*: Pocket Movie Guide
The Peyote Cult
HomeGround: The Kate Bush Anthology
Tim Burton : Hallowe'en For Hollywood
Ken Russell
Cixous, Irigaray, Kristeva: The *Jouissance* of French Feminism
Julia Kristeva: Art, Love, Melancholy, Philosophy, Semiotics and Psychoanalysis
Luce Irigaray: Lips, Kissing, and the Politics of Sexual Difference
Hélène Cixous I Love You: The *Jouissance* of Writing
Andrea Dworkin
'Cosmo Woman': The World of Women's Magazines
Women in Pop Music
Discovering the Goddess (Geoffrey Ashe)
The Poetry of Cinema
The Sacred Cinema of Andrei Tarkovsky
Andrei Tarkovsky: Pocket Guide
Andrei Tarkovsky: *Mirror*: Pocket Movie Guide
Walerian Borowczyk: Cinema of Erotic Dreams
Jean-Luc Godard: The Passion of Cinema
Jean-Luc Godard: Pocket Guide
John Hughes and Eighties Cinema
Ferris Buller's Day Off: Pocket Movie Guide
The Cinema of Richard Linklater
Liv Tyler: Star In Ascendance
Blade Runner and the Films of Philip K. Dick
Paul Bowles and Bernardo Bertolucci
Media Hell: Radio, TV and the Press
Detonation Britain: Nuclear War in the UK
Feminism and Shakespeare
Wild Zones: Pornography, Art and Feminism
Sex in Art: Pornography and Pleasure in Painting and Sculpture
Sexing Hardy: Thomas Hardy and Feminism

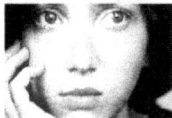

*The Light Eternal is a model monograph, an exemplary job. The subject matter of the book is
beautifully organised and dead on beam.* (Lawrence Durrell)
It is amazing for me to see my work treated with such passion and respect. (Andrea Dworkin)
Sex-Magic-Poetry-Cornwall is a very rich essay... It is like a brightly-lighted box. (Peter Redgrove)

CRESCENT MOON PUBLISHING P.O. Box 1312, Maidstone, Kent, ME14 5XU, Great Britain
0044-1622-729593 cresmopub@yahoo.co.uk www.crmoon.com